This series of books draws on the practical knowledge that the Center for Creative Leadership (CCL®) has generated, since its inception in 1970, through its research and educational activity conducted in partnership with hundreds of thousands of managers and executives. Much of this knowledge is shared— in a way that is distinct from the typical university department, professional association, or consultancy. CCL is not simply a collection of individual experts, although the individual credentials of its staff are impressive; rather it is a community, with its members holding certain principles in common and working together to understand and generate practical responses to today's leadership and organizational challenges. The purpose of the series is to provide managers with specific advice on how to complete a developmental task or solve a leadership challenge. In doing that, the series carries out CCL's mission to advance the understanding, practice, and development of leadership for the benefit of society worldwide. We think you will find the Ideas Into Action Series an important addition to your leadership toolkit.

Michael T. Mitchell serves as senior faculty at the Center for Creative Leadership and is responsible for a variety of open enrollment programs. For a diverse portfolio of custom clients, Mike is involved in early discovery, development, and program delivery. Additionally, he advises CCL's portfolio of clients on all aspects of innovation, including innovation leadership. Mike holds a PhD in organizational leadership from The Chicago School of Psychology and an MBA from Xavier University in Cincinnati, Ohio.

Special thanks to Cathleen Clerkin and David Magellan Horth for reviewing an early version of this work.

SUPPORTING
INNOVATORS
Trust, Purpose, Partnership

Michael T. Mitchell

First edition published 2018.

978-1-60491-875-5 – Print

978-1-60491-876-2 - Ebook

CCL. No. 00469

Cataloging-in-publication data on file with the Library of Congress.

Published by Center for Creative Leadership
CCL Press

Manager, Publication Development: Peter Scisco
Editor: Shaun Martin
Rights and Permissions: Kelly Lombardino
   https://www.ccl.org/permission-republish-request/

Writer: Mark Tosczak
Design and Layout: Carly Bell

CONTENTS

THREE PILLARS OF INNOVATION LEADERSHIP

*When we are creating we are at our most human.
When we are at our most human, we are
at our most vulnerable.*

Most companies and their leaders consider innovation vital. In a 2015 Center for Creative Leadership (CCL) survey of leaders, 94 percent told us just that. But those same leaders also admitted that most of their organizations aren't very good at it. Just 14 percent said their companies were effective innovators.

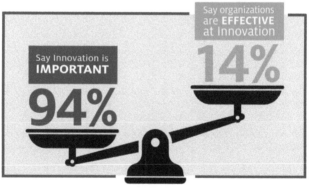

Say organizations are **EFFECTIVE** at Innovation
14%

Say Innovation is **IMPORTANT**
94%

Source: CCL panel of 500 executives

The companies most successful at innovation bridge the gulf between the value of innovation and their capacity to do it effectively—the knowing-doing gap. While there are myriad factors involved in innovation, CCL research has found five keys that separate champion innovators from the rest.

Organizations good at innovation have:

- leaders supporting innovation

- leaders who create a culture that supports innovation

- a formal innovation strategy

- a budget set aside for innovation

- a clear direction for innovation efforts

The first and second of those characteristics—leaders supporting innovation and a culture supporting innovation—speak to how a leader interacts with those responsible for driving innovation efforts—innovators and innovation teams. Leaders responsible for innovation must understand that how they lead is a crucial component of innovation success. In CCL surveys, 80 percent of leaders agree that leading innovation is different from leading other kinds of business activity. Innovation leadership requires many of the same disciplines required to lead operations, but the constant ambiguity, risk, and need for creativity require special attention to emotional intelligence and sensitivity. Those factors are the difference between competent and great innovation leadership.

Leading day-to-day operations involves well-understood

practices in finance, strategy, management, and leadership of the business. Other executives and companies have walked these leadership paths before. Operational leaders know how to support those they lead by securing resources for them, protecting them from disruptive forces, and selling ideas "up" a company's organization chart. They also understand business elements such as finance, strategy, and management practices, and that case studies, company history, and industry best practices provide information that can guide the decisions of leaders at every level.

However, we have found in our research that innovation requires something more from innovation leaders. Innovation, according to CCL, is the creation and implementation of something new that adds value. There is greater ambiguity in innovation work because innovators don't know the exact steps needed for success or what the actual outcome may be. Innovation work is also more visible within the organization (and sometimes outside the organization), and success or failure is quite obvious. These attributes make innovation riskier, more stressful, and more emotionally draining for innovators. However, it's not that good innovation leaders aren't also good operational leaders. Successful innovation leaders acknowledge that both operational and innovation leadership can coexist and seek a delicate balance between them. Leaders should switch between these two modes of leadership thinking in order to help innovators with their work, depending on what the situation requires. Innovation leadership requires that leaders pay special attention to three critical pillars that provide much needed support to innovators and innovation teams: trust, purpose, and partnership.

In identifying these pillars, we relied on extensive interviews with people on the front lines of innovation and their bosses, and we've shared anonymized versions of these interviews later in the book. Our goal was to tease out the essential skills, practices, attitudes, and values of leaders with a track record of multiple innovation successes.

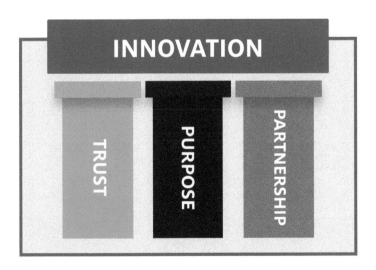

01

Innovation leaders TRUST their innovation teams.
Leaders need to demonstrate, through words and actions, they trust their team's ability to do the work, so that innovators maintain the confidence necessary to succeed.

02

Innovation leaders keep the PURPOSE behind the innovation front and center.
Innovators must stay focused on the "why" that's driving the innovation, even when the path to the goal is difficult to see and/or the goal changes along the way.

03

Innovation leaders PARTNER with the innovators they lead.
The leader's role isn't to come to the table with all the answers or to stand in judgment of the work, but to pitch in as an equal when help is needed.

Developing a new product, business model, technology, or process can be exhilarating and terrifying for innovators, with dramatic ups and downs in their emotions as they move from initial idea to final outcome. To maintain their focus and motivation through such stressful work, innovators need their leaders to support them in three specific ways:

While ideas like trust, purpose, and partnership might seem, at first glance, similar to the practices of many skilled business leaders, they function somewhat differently in innovation. In this book, we present these pillars as three largely distinct practices, but they can overlap in the real world. Sometimes a practice we recommend for communicating trust, such as coaching, can also involve partnering with an innovator or helping a team keep the purpose front and center. Skillful leaders are mindful of all three key pillars as they navigate the day-to-day demands of leading innovation projects.

These pillars of innovation leadership give innovators what they need to be successful: emotional endurance, the space to try new things and make mistakes, and clear focus and direction. Effective innovation leadership tells innovators that their boss is in this effort with them and, whether they succeed or fail, they're not alone. A focus on these three innovation leadership pillars can be critical to filling the knowing-doing gap that separates most of the 94 percent of companies that say innovation is important from the 14 percent that do it effectively.

TRUST THE INNOVATORS

One of the characteristics that distinguishes successful innovation leaders is their trust in their team to successfully innovate, and how they demonstrate that trust in concrete ways. Why is trust so important? Innovators are working to solve a problem for which no one knows the solution, and for which no one is certain to find the answer. Innovators will succeed only if they're confident enough to stretch their abilities as far as they'll go. And they'll only do that if they feel their leaders trust them—even if they make a mistake, encounter failure, and experience the inevitable starts and stops of pursuing innovation.

Without this trust, it's easy for innovators to decide, consciously or not, to play it safe. For instance, they may oversimplify an idea or take out unique and groundbreaking aspects of it. What was the last major innovation you remember that was a result of people doing something predictable and without risk?

Even before finalizing a new innovation, innovators explore many possibilities, with plenty of false starts. Their leaders, whether a manager or an investor backing a new venture, must trust them enough to work through those mistakes and false starts, even if they seem overwhelming. In a 2014 article for *The Globe and Mail*, James Dyson, who eventually built a multi-billion dollar vacuum cleaner company, wrote how he had the idea for a bagless vacuum cleaner in his 30s, but it took him more than 5,127 tries before he finally produced a working model.

Most innovators know their bosses are closely watching their work, and are acutely aware that their success or failure could have a significant impact on their careers. Knowing the stakes they face and that innovation is inherently risky and ambiguous, innovators must have enough grit, passion, and persistence to keep working. They must be willing to keep trying new ideas and exploring new possibilities. In this context, innovators need the trust of their leaders if they're to continue putting forward their best work.

How to Demonstrate Trust

Although it's helpful to innovation team members to hear their leaders say they trust them, words are not enough. In *Leadership Trust*, Christopher Evans writes that to trust someone is to make yourself vulnerable to their actions. In the case of innovation work, it involves making an active choice to risk failure in order to achieve innovations that may have a lasting impact. Trustworthy leaders demonstrate their vulnerability through what they do consistently and what they never do (or do rarely). Leaders should avoid

The Importance of Patience

The process of creating new and useful products, services, etc. is not always a straight and predictable road. There are twists and turns. Organizations that run out of patience too soon tend to get a less than ideal result or crush the innovation team's momentum and commitment. Conversely, organizations that keep expectations high while also exercising patience get better results and maintain the commitment of the innovator/innovation team. For example, one innovation manager we know was working on a difficult product. The company, desperately in need for the potential revenue from this new product, was growing impatient with the difficulties and slow-downs in the development process. The innovation manager presented two options to the organization: The first option guaranteed a faster and reliable path to execution, but would result in a less than novel product. The second option would take longer and was riskier, but could result in a truly novel product. Seeing the wisdom of being patient, and trusting in the innovation manager, the company opted for the second option. Launching a few months late, the product exceeded even the most ambitious sales projections, demonstrating that the organization's patience and trust in the innovation manager paid off.

behaviors that could signal they don't trust the innovator and instead embrace behaviors that tell innovators "I trust that you have the ability to see this project through to successful completion."

There are three behaviors in particular that can harm innovators—signaling to innovators that their leaders don't trust their ability to do the job. These untrusting behaviors are like giant psychological stop signs to innovators. They signal "I don't think you have what it takes" or "I'm not certain you can make this project work out." Facing those perceptions, innovators might slow their work dramatically or perhaps halt altogether.

Micromanaging. When leaders focus too much on unimportant details and are prescriptive in their instructions, it sends a clear message that they don't believe the innovation team can do the job on its own.

Focusing too much (and too negatively) on the problems. If the leader finds and focuses only on problems, it erodes the innovator's confidence. Although innovators must tackle the problems that arise, it's emotionally draining for them to be constantly reminded of obstacles as they seek a way forward. This negative focus signals to the team "Why did you let this happen?" or "You shouldn't have made that decision." Innovators will inevitably make mistakes along the path to innovation. That feeling of blame can be discouraging—the opposite of providing the support innovators need.

Failure to recognize progress. Likewise, as innovators move forward, leaders who don't visibly recognize their

I Know You Can Do This

During our research we met an innovation manager who, while working on a major new product, became discouraged by a snag the project had hit. The package design that had passed consumer testing could not be used due to a possible trademark infringement. The company's legal team had brought things to a screeching halt, and the innovation manager was feeling that all might be lost. In a follow-up meeting with his boss, the manager explained the situation and his sense of lost confidence in his ability to pull the project through this rough patch. The leader made a simple suggestion that demonstrated her trust in his ability to pull through and rebuilt his shaking confidence. She said, "You know better than anyone what this new product needs. There are many other possible package options, and I'm sure you have the right eye for finding a great alternative." The manager responded to this suggestion with renewed confidence, coming back with not just one but three possible solutions. The boss's simple demonstration of confidence in the manager's ability led him to overcome an obstacle, significantly improve the new product idea, and renewed his confidence in his own ability to do the difficult work of innovation.

team's accomplishments communicate that progress doesn't matter and isn't valued. This is a sure way to shake the confidence of innovation teams and weaken their will to continue.

Establishing trust is not just a matter of avoiding trust-harming behaviors, though. Leaders need to actively communicate through their words and behaviors that they trust their teams can produce innovative results. Therefore, they need to seek and find opportunities at key points in the innovation process to let the innovator know "you've got this."

Trust is essential for innovators to feel safe while taking creative risks. By taking the risk that the innovation team may fail, leaders demonstrate the vulnerability needed to establish effective trust. How can a leader demonstrate the kind of powerful trust that innovators need to do their best work? Here are three techniques that any leader can start using immediately to demonstrate and amplify the trust they feel for their innovators.

Coaching

CCL believes that leadership is a collaborative process involving all members of a group—not just the person at the top. This idea is critical for innovation. Leaders don't always know how to accomplish a particular innovation goal. That's why there's typically a team of people working on the problem. A coaching approach, where leaders ask questions and solicit expertise and ideas, gives team members the clear message that they have what it takes. Effective coaching also involves listening for more than just the facts of the innovation problem, however. Pay attention to feelings and values, which are harder to listen for but may provide key insights into what innovators are really dealing with.

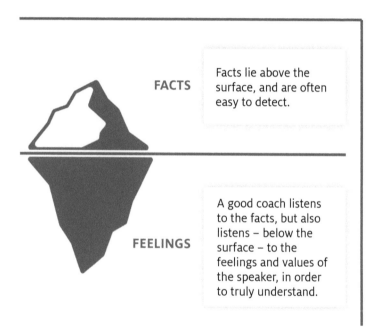

FACTS

Facts lie above the surface, and are often easy to detect.

FEELINGS

A good coach listens to the facts, but also listens – below the surface – to the feelings and values of the speaker, in order to truly understand.

When coaching an innovator, here are five things to keep in mind according to CCL's *Better Conversations Every Day*, a one-day experience designed to help leaders develop coaching skills applicable across the organization. ➡

01 **Avoid problem solving.** The person you're coaching is the one responsible for the doing the work, not you. If you take over the work, you'll send a message that you don't trust this person.

02 **Coach the person, not the problem.** Coach the person, not the problem. Chances are, those you're coaching know more about the actual challenge than you do. Your task in coaching is to help those them be more effective, so they can solve this problem and future challenges on their own.

03 **Ask open, honest questions.** Even if you think you might know the answer to a particular question or problem, a better approach is to ask open, honest questions and see what those you're coaching think. By avoiding leading innovators to a particular answer, you communicate your belief that the innovators know the answer or can figure it out on their own.

04 **Ask powerful questions.** Open-ended queries such as "Can you imagine if this idea were bigger?", or "What would success look or feel like?" can free innovators to see greater possibilities. Asking innovators to rate a problem or opportunity on a scale from small to large can help bring perspective to a situation.

05 **Listen!** Ask questions rather than give advice. You should be talking less than 30 percent of the time. This focus on what the innovator or innovation team is saying sends a message that you care what team members think, feel, and value.

In a coaching relationship, your goal is to help others be more effective in finding solutions to the problems they face, which will lead to team members who can perform at a high level over the long term and who feel that you trust them.

Appreciative Inquiry

Too often, leaders are tempted to identify problems and to focus on what's not working. Appreciative inquiry turns that on its head. It's a way to focus on positive achievement, energizing people by making them feel that they're valued and making progress. How does it work?

STEP 01 | **Define:** Agree on the topic of the conversation. For innovators it might be "What have we accomplished since the last status update?"

STEP 02 | **Discover:** Solicit what positive discoveries or solutions (even if they're not complete) have been made, both recently and since the project has started. Help innovators recognize this progress.

STEP 03 | **Dream:** Use the successes described during step two to imagine with the team what could be and where the next steps might lead you and the innovation team.

STEP 04 | **Design:** Based on past successes and future possibilities, open the conversation to discuss what the innovation team should work on next and what it should try to achieve.

| STEP 05 | **Deliver**: As a result of your discussion, work with the team to define what it will work on achieving or will deliver during the next phase of work. |

Because appreciative inquiry focuses on positives and is forward-looking and collaborative in nature, innovators get the message loud and clear from their leader: "You are making great strides, and I trust that you'll continue to make progress!"

Delegation

When leaders delegate, they communicate their trust in the people they lead. Delegation can boost confidence, allowing innovators to take the bigger—but important—risks required for creating something new.

Delegation injects new energy into innovators, and is one of the most powerful trust-building tools leaders have in their toolbox. When leaders delegate to their team or individual team members, they demonstrate confidence in that person or group's ability to do something. Confidence is important for innovators to maintain, even when they're in a low point innovation work often provokes. Leaders should delegate often when working with innovators, though they must also recognize when to engage more directly with a team or individuals.

Here are some tips for delegating to the innovators you lead:

- **Start small.** If you do not have full confidence in your people, have them take on just one task and assess their performance before giving them greater responsibility.

- **Share the context for each assignment you delegate.** What is its history? Who is invested in its satisfactory completion? Who will evaluate the work, and how will they do that? What are some likely obstacles? Tell people what you know.

- **Communicate your assumptions.** Convey how you think the work might be done. Give people the benefit of your knowledge, but don't insist it's the way the work must be done. Invite them to suggest improvements to your approach.

- **Tell people how and when you'll check in.** Set the expectation that you'll follow up, so when you do, it's not a surprise or misinterpreted as micromanaging.

- **Take stock of your team's talents.** Know what skills team members bring to the job. Learn more about their experiences on this job and from previous jobs.

- **Know your team's passions.** What do team members aspire to? What do they value? What excites them? If you do not know, ask. Find the intersection of talent and passion—let people apply their best skills to work that they find most energizing.

- **Have a backup plan.** Treat delegation as a test. You want to see whether another person can take on a challenge and handle it well. Be prepared to get personally involved or assign someone else to the work if the person
assigned isn't up to the task.

- **Be prepared for failure.** Treat failure as an opportunity for team members to learn, not as an excuse for you to punish them.

- **Close the assignment.** When the person assigned the task completes the work, ask what was learned, provide some feedback and affirmation, and then take the opportunity to talk about the next assignment.

Leaders depend on their innovation teams to do the challenging, creative work that leads to products and ideas that can transform companies and, sometimes, entire industries. During low points in this work, innovators need support to maintain their confidence, emotional energy, and creativity. How leaders communicate that they believe in innovators' ability to overcome obstacles and produce a successful innovation is essential for maintaining the drive to innovate.

KEEP INNOVATORS FOCUSED ON THE PURPOSE

Innovation isn't creativity for its own sake. Rather, organizations undertake innovation efforts to achieve specific goals. Those may be as dramatic as a tech industry titan's dream to put humans on Mars or as mundane as a new kind of shampoo. Whatever it is, the innovators involved must keep that purpose front and center.

However, it's not uncommon for goals to change during the course of an innovation project. Perhaps there's a fortune to be made in asteroid mining instead of colonizing Mars, or maybe the new shampoo would work better as a skin lotion. But whether the goal is fixed or evolves as the team makes new discoveries and generates new ideas, it's critical that team members remain focused on it. Even when the innovation team is confident they have the trust of their leader, if they're not certain the project itself is the right project, they can lose motivation and inspiration.

Keeping purpose front and center is a vital component of the support leaders must provide to innovators. That's because innovators need not only a clear sense of purpose, they also need inspiration. When there are the inevitable changes and alterations, and the creative well temporarily runs dry, inspiration can keep innovators going.

So how can leaders keep purpose front and center with their innovation teams? These three approaches may be helpful:

1. linking innovation to organizational strategy

2. vision setting

3. framing and reframing

Linking Innovation to Organizational Strategy

The purpose of an innovation may be to change the course of human history, like establishing a settlement on another planet, or something much more practical, like creating a new shampoo. But whatever the project's scope, it's key for leaders to answer the question *What's in it for our organization?* In other words, how the innovation either fits into the company's goals and strategies or has the potential to take the company in a completely new direction (and why that's a good thing!).

Communicating this might be as simple as reiterating an organization's goals or strategy. Innovators have probably heard this information before, but they may have lost sight of the connection between what they read in a corporate memo or heard at a company town hall meeting

❝ Going over goals and strategy with innovators is a perfect opportunity to use appreciative inquiry, to connect actions with purpose. ❞

and their innovation work. In addition, leaders can spend time with innovators going over those goals and strategy in greater detail. This time can help innovators clarify the link between their work and organizational goals and help them see how an innovation project fits in with other company activities.

Finally, an innovation leader can bring in others, even other senior leaders, to help connect the day-to-day work of innovation and the organization's strategic goals and plan. This can help align innovation resources, including the emotional buy-in of individuals and the team, with the organization's strategy. Effective leaders stay alert for signs that innovators are losing sight of the purpose or losing faith in its value. When they see innovators drifting off course, they work to put them back on the path toward meaningful innovation.

Vision in Action

Here's one example of how stating and restating the vision behind an innovation inspired a team to keep working through adversity. A food company was trying to develop some new products based around a homemade, farm-to-table approach—products that would be healthy and good for consumers. But the new product team was struggling and had lost sight of the inspiring purpose behind the project.

During a meeting the group started to get very negative, clearly feeling defeated. Their boss stopped them and laid out, in an eloquent and compelling way, why the company was pursuing this. She used colorful, inspiring language to paint a picture and vision of the consumer the company was trying to reach and what the company wanted to do for her—"That single parent, who's working and trying to put good stuff in the lunch box for their kids, but can't afford Whole Foods."

The team had gotten lost in the details, but this leader's colorful and accurate vision for the project's purpose helped them refocus on an inspiring call to action. It was the boost the team needed to get back on track.

Vision Setting

Even if an innovation team understands how its project connects to the bigger picture for the organization, the team still may have trouble seeing exactly what it's trying to achieve as its work progresses, or the team may feel that the project simply isn't that interesting or even innovative.

When this happens, leaders can help to remind the innovation team of the vision for the project. While the course to successful innovation is unpredictable, the vision driving the innovation should be clear. Skillful leaders devote time and energy to making sure those they lead can "see" the destination and understand the new reality the organization is trying to create.

This goes beyond communicating how an innovation effort fits into a company's strategy. It's about developing a vision of what success looks like. When Apple's engineers and designers were working on the first iPhone, their vision was simple: Put an iPod and a phone in the same device. Apple executives thought most people wouldn't carry both a music player and a phone, so they wanted to offer a device with both capabilities. Later, the vision expanded to include a device that was always connected to the internet. When Steve Jobs unveiled the iPhone in 2007, he described it by saying "Today, we're introducing three revolutionary products..."

The vision of combining three distinct functions in a single, elegantly designed device was revolutionary. Although even Jobs didn't anticipate how the iPhone, and the App Store that followed it, would launch a mobile internet revolution and give rise to a whole new ecosystem of companies.

Vision setting is a powerful and inspiring tool for innovators. But is it still useful if the purpose of the innovation changes or evolves during the process? Yes. In fact, when the purpose shifts for an innovation project, leaders should consider helping the group to reestablish the vision to help keep the energy and excitement of innovators high, even as they abandon some possibilities and adopt new ones.

Framing and Reframing

Innovation is not a straight line from goal to execution. Leaders must prepare for the inevitable setbacks and detours that lead innovators astray. Framing (or reframing when a goal changes) can help innovators see their challenge more clearly and see it in a new light that may suggest different solutions. Furthermore, such reframing can help keep a team focused on their original purpose, especially when they encounter a problem that could end up distracting or derailing their focus. To help frame the purpose of an innovation, leaders can ask powerful questions or ask innovators to rethink the fundamental questions considered, challenge assumptions, and bring in multiple perspectives.

One method of framing and reframing we recommend is a technique called the "Five Whys" methodology, originally developed in the 1930s by Sakichi Toyoda of Toyota

Industries. This is a technique for thinking through a problem to get a clearer view of the challenge involved and generate potential solutions. Participants start with asking why a simple premise or problem is important, and then asking why the answer is important, and then asking why that answer is important, and so on. The objective is to achieve more clarity with each successive answer.

Here's how that might work a company trying to launch a new brand of loose leaf tea after receiving negative feedback from consumers.

> Why is our new brand of tea not selling well? Research shows consumers don't like the flavor of our new beverage product.

> Why don't they like the flavor? Because it makes their throats feel dry after drinking it.

> Why does it make their throats feel dry? Because it's too acidic.

> Why is it too acidic? Because the acidity balances the sweetness.

> Why do we need to balance the sweetness? Because customers prefer tea that isn't overly sweet.

POSSIBLE SOLUTION: Are there other ways to balance the sweetness while reducing the acidity? Perhaps we lower the sugar content?

The team has now moved from a problem to a way forward. Using the Five Whys, the team reframed the problem, digging into a series of "whys" that allowed them to understand the problem better and then come up with potential solutions. This keeps the team focused and moving forward.

PARTNER WITH INNOVATORS

In our interviews with innovation leaders and the teams they lead we found partnering was a crucial differentiator between successful and unsuccessful innovation projects. Leaders demonstrate partnering in their willingness to share in the work, rewards, and failures as an equal member of the team. Leaders demonstrate partnering when they contribute to the progress of the innovation as an equal— not as someone with better ideas or the final word. Leaders demonstrate partnering when they are willing to use their authority to obtain what the team needs from someone in their position: resources, time, patience from senior management, appreciation for the difficulty of the work from the various stakeholders, etc. Ultimately, the leader needs to demonstrate a willingness to put their own reputation on the line for the idea. If their followers are willing to stake their careers on the outcome of the innovation, the leader needs to show they are willing to go into that battle with them.

Here are three ways leaders can partner with their innovation teams:

- leveraging authority to provide practical assistance

- ideation

- flipping the boss role

Each of these is different, but each provides leaders concrete ways to help a project succeed by partnering with those doing the day-to-day work of innovation.

Leveraging Authority to Provide Practical Assistance

Some of the most valuable things a leader can do are the same things that leaders do in other roles. For innovation projects, these include obtaining resources, such as money, specific expertise, or assistance from others in the organization to support the team. Leaders can also provide substantial help to innovators by serving as their connection with other parts of the organization. This might mean protecting innovators from undue outside interference, while at other times it might mean selling the innovators' idea to senior management or to other parts of the organization.

This may seem mundane. After all, don't leaders often provide assistance to their followers in day-to-day operations? Yes, but that's all the more reason to emphasize it here. While there are many things that are unique to

Becoming a Champion

A product manager we worked with had the habit of arriving at work early in the morning, before everybody else. One morning the CEO, also an early starter, stopped in his office and said, "Tell me what you're working on."

It was a little intimidating for the product manager, who didn't want to risk saying the wrong thing. But with just the two of them there early in the morning, there was no way to avoid the conversation, so the product manager risked being vulnerable and showed the CEO what he was working on. His vulnerability was rewarded. The CEO became really engaged with the idea. In fact, he became a champion for that product and became a sort of partner to the product manager.

The CEO wasn't there every day, but when a big snag came along, he would ask if he could lend his authority or resources to help the new product team. He was willing to help when he could, but he didn't impose on the innovators. For the product manager, it felt like the CEO was just as committed as he was. The product ended up being a huge success.

Of course, not every innovator will have the opportunity to have the CEO support them so directly. But all leaders can think about their role in supporting innovation like the CEO did—by demonstrating partnership and becoming a true champion of the idea.

leading innovation projects, it's important to remember that some of the basic leadership functions remain the same.

Ideation

Sometimes innovators simply need more brains in the room. Leaders can be powerful allies by participating in ideation (new idea creation) sessions with innovators. To be clear, leaders are not participating in ideation sessions because they know more or have better ideas. They're participating because, at key points in the innovation process, there's significant value that can be gained by generating a wide range of new ideas and approaches. Leaders, in this context, must take pains to act as an equal and a peer to others in the room. Their ideas may not be better than others' (in fact, they probably won't be), but a leader, just like anyone, brings different perspectives into the creative space in which innovations are generated.

During ideation work, leaders should take care that their ideas aren't treated any differently than anyone else's. Likewise, they shouldn't criticize others' ideas or judge them too soon. Early criticism of new ideas is one of the most potent killers of innovation, and leaders must remember that new ideas are often especially vulnerable to criticism simply because there hasn't been enough time and energy put into fleshing them out.

Flipping the Boss Role

Finally, there are times during the innovation process

when the best thing a leader can do is ask the team "What can I do to help you?" The answer might sometimes be as simple as "Give us more time." Other times it might be a request for specific resources or input. By putting themselves at the disposal of the team, leaders send a strong signal that they are an equal member of the team, willing to pitch in in any way. However, remember that partnering is not the act of giving up on the boss role; rather it is about using one's skills, knowledge, and authority to help innovators overcome challenges. A leader who gives up on the boss role can appear withdrawn from the innovation work, leaving their team feeling vulnerable and confused. skills, knowledge, and authority to help innovators overcome challenges. A leader who gives up on the boss role can appear withdrawn from the innovation work, leaving their team feeling vulnerable and confused.

Dealing with the Politics

We once met a manager in a big agricultural commodity marketing organization who had a radical, innovative idea. This organization gets its funding from farmers—some from the small number of really big producers, some from the large number of smaller producers. There's a lot of politics involved in managing these various groups and keeping everyone happy. So, this person went to his boss to tell him about this idea, which would radically change how their organization would do their business.

Instead of grilling him on the business case, focusing on the internal political issues, or immediately jumping to the pitfalls of implementation, his boss said, "How can I help you?" Even though the idea was so radical that she herself didn't fully understand it, she trusted the manager, and knew that he needed support and partnering to get his idea off the ground. She recognized there would be a lot of pushback from farmers and she took on the role of managing the politics of the idea. She saw that her title, role, and the respect she enjoyed among farmers would allow her to influence the process in a way this innovator couldn't. He could concentrate on innovation, and she could make sure politics didn't get in the way.

In this case, the leader recognized her strengths and what role she could play, and she embraced that role, clearing the way for the innovator to do his job.

OVERCOME OBSTACLES

We've laid out an effective approach for leaders responsible for innovation, based on evidence of what's worked for many organizations and individuals. Remember that each of the three innovation leadership pillars we've presented here are complementary. Take away one of them and your innovation efforts may slow down, produce unimpressive results, or fail entirely.

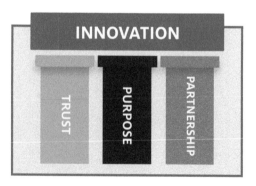

For example, if trust and partnership are present, but purpose is missing, innovators and their leader may have a good working relationship and the team may be busy, but may be unlikely to know why they are working or what they are working toward, and may lose their way.

If trust and purpose are present but partnership is missing, innovators may move forward but limit their risk taking. Without partnership, they won't feel confident that they'll be supported if they make mistakes, so they won't be put themselves in a vulnerable position by bringing issues or problems forward. This can drive them toward "safe" advances, lowering the potential positive impact of innovation.

Finally, if purpose and partnership are present, but trust is absent, progress is likely to be slow. In this case, innovators are likely to move forward only in fits and starts, as they won't feel confident in their own ability to make real progress.

Of course, it would be nice if these three pillars were all that were needed for the success of innovation efforts. But innovation isn't that simple. In addition to the sheer uncertainty of any innovation by itself, many leaders will also face organizational challenges. From the difficulty of navigating corporate politics to organizational leadership that doesn't understand what innovation really means, sometimes threats to innovation come from outside the innovation team and its leader.

Educating bosses, peers, and key influencers about the value of innovation and how to best manage it is valuable, but not always possible. Here are some common challenges that innovation leaders may face, and some suggestions on how to approach them: an inability to embrace innovation, and corporate politics and power shifts.

Inability to Embrace Innovation

Many organizations and leaders say they want innovation, but find it difficult to truly embrace the slow, ambiguous process involved. For instance, some corporate cultures value speed in decision making and action—lean methodology is one example of prioritizing speed, with its focus on continuous improvement and the elimination of inefficiencies in the development process. Rapid development processes may seem to contradict the slow, ambiguous nature of innovation. However, organizations successful at innovation face similar roadblocks all the time. Rather than barriers that must be overcome, these roadblocks are tensions that organizations must manage and balance. Understanding the needs of day-to-day operations, the needs of your innovation team, and how to balance both, is crucial. The key here is setting expectations. Using examples and case studies from other companies, for example, leaders can explain that because of its unpredictability, innovation can take longer than many other operations-focused initiatives. Leaders should also secure commitments for sufficient time for innovators to show some progress, without having to guarantee a final result on a given deadline.

Leaders may find it valuable to negotiate gateways for the innovation project—periodic reviews as it advances, with a formal process for deciding whether or not it should proceed through each gateway. In pharmaceutical development, for example, this approach is common, with gateways established based on laboratory, pre-clinical, and clinical trial results.

Another common obstacle to embracing innovation is risk aversion. Innovation involves doing things that have uncertain and ambiguous outcomes—the very definition of risk. One way to manage risk is through rapid prototyping. Rapid prototyping is a process of building a model that represents what the actual finished product or process might look like (and it plays a big role in lean methodology and other rapid-development techniques). Using a prototype is a less expensive and less risky way to get feedback on an idea before proceeding to full production. A prototype can also help garner internal support and understanding, which can help mitigate risk of a new idea.

Leaders can also incorporate more testing, pilot projects, and customer research into innovation efforts. By getting more information earlier, leaders can reduce perceived risks.

Corporate Politics and Power Shifts

Innovation tends to be a high-profile process. Even during the most secret innovation projects, senior leaders and board members are probably watching. The high-profile nature of innovation makes it, and the leaders responsible, vulnerable to corporate politics.

Corporate politics often appear as conflicts over goals

and resources within an organization or as concerns about how innovation might have a negative effect on some people or functions. An innovation leader who understands the concerns of those opposed to innovation can move to either secure their support or at least neutralize it with top decision makers.

Some executives may be concerned about how an innovation project is changing spending or investment decisions, even before there's a clear outcome. In other cases, leaders may worry that an innovation could dramatically shift power among different business units and product lines, threatening their budgets, compensation, or career ambitions. For example, consider how the role of the chief technology officer or chief information officer has expanded dramatically in the last 25 years, reshaping power in the C-suite.

Leaders should be aware of how their projects might shift power within an organization, and then take steps to proactively manage any potential fallout. For example, leaders could meet with executives in the organization that might be negatively affected and find ways to engage them in the process—perhaps by finding ways that innovation could strengthen their business units. Again, successful innovation leadership requires balancing the needs of day-to-day operations and the needs of your innovation team. Part of that balance will require you to successfully navigate (and help guide your team through) the corporate politics that could derail your innovation efforts.)

Your Turn

Innovation (and innovation leadership) is risky, stressful, and emotionally draining. It therefore requires a different (and specific) implementation of the leadership skills you have developed over your career. The three pillars we've explained in this book—trust, keeping purpose front and center, and partnering—are effective ways to support innovation efforts. We know from experience that these pillars work. They distinguish the great innovators and their leaders from everyone else.

Sometimes, building these pillars is simple. Small daily actions, like a few words or even your body language in a meeting, add up over time and make a positive difference in how innovators feel about themselves and their work. Other times, building these pillars carry risk, such as when you're facing pressure from your boss, and your team is stuck with a tough problem and not making much progress. The work of innovation itself may feel ambiguous, since it pushes your team into unexplored territory with your team's innovation efforts. Remember the three pillars. You and your innovators are in this together, and only by supporting your innovators can you succeed in helping to create great innovations.

Suggested Resources

Center for Creative Leadership (2018). *Better conversations every day: Facilitator guide.* Greensboro, NC: Center for Creative Leadership.https://www.ccl.org/leadership-solutions/coaching-services/better-conversations-every-day/

Clerkin, C., & Cullen-Lester, K. (2015). *Navigating innovation roadblocks: Key differences between innovative and non-innovative organizations* [White paper]. Retrieved from https://www.ccl.org/wp-content/uloads/2015/08/navigating-innovation-roadblocks.pdf

Evans, C. (2015). *Leadership trust: Build it, keep it.* Greensboro, NC: Center for Creative Leadership.

Gryskiewicz, S., & Taylor, S. (2003). *Making creativity practical: Innovation that gets results.* Greensboro, NC: Center for Creative Leadership.

Hoppe, M. (2014). *Active listening: Improve your ability to listen and lead.* Greensboro, NC: Center for Creative Leadership.

Horth, D., & Buchner, C. (2014). *Innovation leadership: How to use innovation to lead effectively, work collaboratively, and drive results* [White paper]. Retrieved from https://www.ccl.org/wp-content/uploads/2015/04/InnovationLeadership.pdf

Horth, D.M., & Mitchell, M. (2017). *How to treat new Ideas.* Greensboro, NC: Center for Creative Leadership.

Horth, D.M., and Vehar, J. (2014). *Becoming a leader who fosters innovation* [White paper]. Retrieved from https://www.ccl.org/wp-content/uploads/2014/03/BecomingLeaderFostersInnovation.pdf

Mitchell, M. (2017). *3 crucial behaviors for successfully leading innovation* [White paper]. Retrieved from https://www.ccl.org/wp-content/uloads/2017/08/3-Crucial-Behaviors-Successfully-Leading-Innovation.pdf

Scisco, P., Biech, E., and Hallenbeck, G. (2017). Delegating. In *Compass: Your guide for leadership development and coaching* (pp. 169-176). Greensboro, NC: Center for Creative Leadership.